# Mysteries of the Rosary

**Michael O'Neill McGrath,** OSFS

WORLD LIBRARY PUBLICATIONS

Franklin Park, Illinois

*Mysteries of the Rosary* © 2008, World Library Publications,
the music and liturgy division of J. S. Paluch Company, Inc.
3708 River Road, Suite 400, Franklin Park, Illinois 60131-2158
800 566-6150 • www.wlpmusic.com

Art and commentary by Michael O'Neill McGrath © 2008, World Library Publications.

Photograph by Mark Winterbottom, Copyright © Mark Winterbottom.
Used with permission.

The paintings were done in acrylics on watercolor paper.

This book was edited by Christine Krzystofczyk with assistance from
Alan J. Hommerding and Marcia T. Lucey. Design and layout by Christine Enault.
Production manager was Deb Johnston. The book was set in Berkeley Oldstyle,
Berliner Grotesk, and Adobe Garamond. Printed in the United States.
Graphics TwoFortyFour Inc.

WLP 017344    ISBN 978-1-58459-402-4

# Mysteries
## of the
## Rosary

This book belongs to

_____

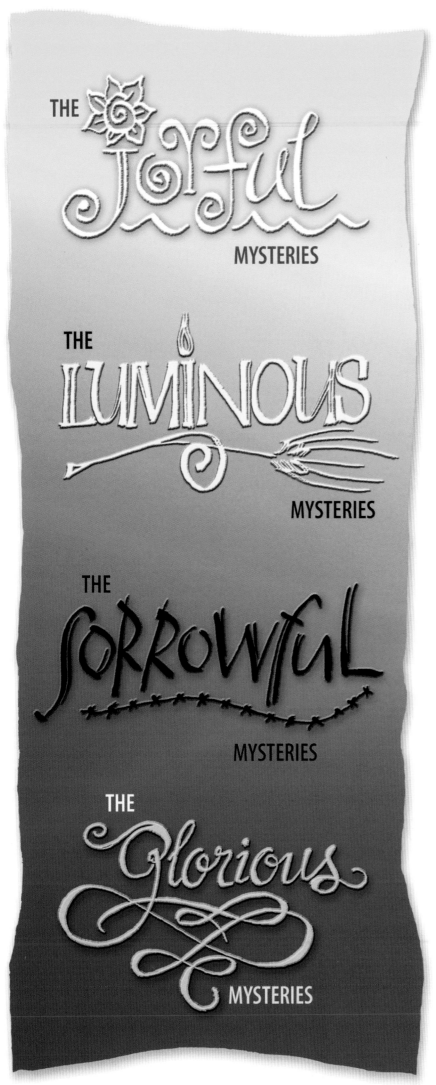

THE **Joyful** MYSTERIES

The Annunciation

The Visitation

The Nativity

The Presentation

The Finding in the Temple

THE **LUMINOUS** MYSTERIES

The Baptism of Jesus

The Wedding at Cana

The Proclamation of the Kingdom

The Transfiguration

The Eucharist

THE **SORROWFUL** MYSTERIES

The Agony in the Garden

The Scourging of Jesus

Jesus Is Crowned with Thorns

The Carrying of the Cross

The Crucifixion

THE **Glorious** MYSTERIES

The Resurrection

The Ascension

Pentecost

The Assumption of Mary

Mary Is Crowned Queen of Heaven

# The Mysteries of the Rosary

## By Michael O'Neill McGrath

This book is about holy mysteries, or stories from the life of Jesus and Mary that help us to pray. There are four sets of mysteries: joyful, luminous, sorrowful, and glorious. When we pray the rosary, the mysteries reflect the many ways in which stories from the life of Jesus can remind us of stories from our own life. We make these connections through colors and symbols.

One good way to learn the mysteries is to see how they relate to different seasons of the church year, just like the calendar seasons of winter, spring, summer, and fall. The liturgical seasons of the church year are connected to prayer and worship, or liturgy. We see the colors change in church and on the priest's vestments when the seasons change, just as we wear different clothes when the seasons of nature change.

Artists use symbols in their paintings to help us understand these mysteries better. This book will help you learn how certain colors or objects make it easier to remember events from the life of Jesus or why the colors change in church in different seasons.

One last thing: Since we believe that all people are made in the image and likeness of God, you will notice that each set of mysteries shows us a different culture. This is because Jesus told the first apostles to bring his message to every nation in the whole world. It's a good and holy thing for artists to depict Jesus and Mary as people from every land and race so that everyone can see them that way, too. That's why we call the Church universal!

# THE Joyful MYSTERIES

## Stories from the Childhood of Jesus

If you were ever born (and since you are reading this book, it's a safe bet that you were), then that's a good reason for you to celebrate the joyful mysteries. They are the stories about Jesus' birth and childhood that are celebrated during Advent and Christmas. In church, we see violet for Advent and white and gold for Christmas. This is a season to enjoy lots of bright, joyful colors like the lights on a Christmas tree.

In the depictions of the joyful mysteries, we see sunflowers and a big sun hat on Mary's head, like a halo. Sunflowers are big, bold flowers that bend toward the sun. Since Jesus is the Light of the world, the sun is a perfect symbol for him.

What colors and shapes make you think of joy?

Luke 1:26–33, 38

**The Annunciation**
The angel Gabriel announces the good news to Mary
that she is to be the mother of Jesus.

Luke 1:39–45

**The Visitation**

Mary visits her cousin Elizabeth to share the good news of two miraculous births—
Jesus and John the Baptist.

**The Nativity**
Jesus is born in a stable in Bethlehem.

Luke 2:6-12

Luke 2:22–32

**The Presentation**
Mary and Joseph bring Jesus to the Temple to present him to God
and have him blessed by Simeon and Anna.

**The Finding in the Temple**

Mary and Joseph thought Jesus was lost in Jerusalem,
but they found him preaching to the elders in the Temple.

Luke 2:41–50

# THE LUMINOUS MYSTERIES

## Stories of Jesus' Ministry on Earth

The luminous mysteries teach us about the ministry, or work, of Jesus when he was an adult. Even though he was God, he was also an ordinary human being who loved to mingle with ordinary people like us. He told them stories and worked miracles for them. In these paintings, we connect the luminous mysteries to Ordinary Time in the liturgical year, symbolized by the color green in church. Since luminous means "full of light," yellow and orange are good symbols to remind us that God's light fills our most ordinary times, like wedding receptions or hiking up a mountain with friends.

What ordinary things do you do that make you think of Jesus?

**The Baptism of Jesus**

John the Baptist baptizes Jesus in the River Jordan.

Luke 2:41–50

John 2:1–11

**The Wedding at Cana**
Jesus performs his first miracle at a wedding reception.

**The Proclamation of the Kingdom**
Jesus explains what it means to follow him.

Mark 1:14–15

Matthew 17:1–8

**The Transfiguration**
Jesus appears in his glory with Moses and Elijah to three apostles.

Matthew 26:26–28

**The Eucharist**
Jesus offers the gift of his body and blood in bread and wine at the Last Supper.

# THE SORROWFUL MYSTERIES

**Stories of the Suffering and Death of Jesus**

If you have ever experienced illness or death in your family, or anything else that made you very sad, the sorrowful mysteries remind you that you are not alone because Jesus knows all about suffering and will stay by your side. The colors of Lent and Holy Week are purple and red, so we will see lots of those colors to remind us of blood and bruises. Purple comes from mixing blue, the color of heaven, with red, the color of earth. Even our saddest days are mixed with the love of God.

What colors make you feel sad? How can you help someone who is feeling sad?

**The Agony in the Garden**

Jesus prays for strength the night before he dies.

Luke 22:39–46

Mark 15:6–15

**The Scourging of Jesus**
Roman soldiers beat and torture Jesus.

**Jesus Is Crowned with Thorns**

John 19:1–8

Soldiers make a crown out of thorns to mock Jesus and call him king.

Luke 23:26–32

**The Carrying of the Cross**
Jesus' friends weep for him as he carries his cross to Calvary.

**The Crucifixion**

Jesus dies on the cross.

John 19:25–30

# THE *Glorious* MYSTERIES

### Stories of Jesus and Mary in Heaven

The glorious mysteries remind us that we will live forever with Jesus, Mary, and all the saints in heaven after we die. During the Easter season, the church is filled with white and gold, the colors of lilies and daffodils, the colors of spring. We also see bright colors like Easter eggs and blooming flowers everywhere. The color red on Pentecost reminds us of the fire of the Holy Spirit. And here's the best part: We don't have to wait until we get to heaven to see Jesus because the glory of God's love is all around us every day.

What people and things remind you of God's love every day?

Mark 16:1–7

**The Resurrection**
Jesus rises to life on Easter morning after dying on Good Friday.

Luke 24:45–53

**The Ascension**
Jesus returns to his Father in heaven.

**Pentecost**

Acts 2:1–7, 11

The Holy Spirit appears in tongues of flame
to inspire the followers of Jesus—including us today.

Luke 1:46–55

**The Assumption of Mary**
Mary is taken up to heaven, body and soul.

Revelation 12:1; Judith 13:18–20

**Mary Is Crowned Queen of Heaven**
Mary leads the angels, saints, and all of us in praising God for eternity.

## How to Say the Rosary

- Begin on the crucifix and say the Apostles' Creed.

- On the first bead, say one Our Father.

- On each of the next three beads, say the Hail Mary.

- Next say one Glory Be. Then think about the first mystery in the group of mysteries you'll be praying and say one Our Father.

- On each of the next ten beads, say one Hail Mary. Follow these with one Glory Be.

- Repeat previous step for each of the five mysteries in the group you are praying.

# ABOUT THE ROSARY

The rosary has been one of the best-loved and most highly revered prayers in the Church for many centuries. Since it is a prayer form that honors Mary, it entails saying the Hail Mary fifty times while meditating on the life of Jesus.

There are many types of rosaries made of a wide variety of materials, from plastic to glass to wood. There are even some you can wear as a ring on your finger. But the one pictured here is the most common type. It has one crucifix, one medal of Jesus or Mary, and some larger beads for the Our Father. Most of the beads, though, are the smaller ones that help us keep count of the many times we pray the words of the Hail Mary.

The colors of this rosary are in keeping with the sections of this book, each decade displaying the colors of the liturgical seasons.

## Apostles' Creed

I believe in God, the Father almighty,
creator of heaven and earth.

I believe in Jesus Christ, his only Son, our Lord.
    He was conceived by the power of the Holy Spirit
        and born of the Virgin Mary.
    He suffered under Pontius Pilate,
        was crucified, died, and was buried.
    He descended to the dead.
    On the third day he rose again.
    He ascended into heaven,
        and is seated at the right hand of the Father.
    He will come again to judge the living and the dead.

I believe in the Holy Spirit,
    the holy catholic Church,
    the communion of saints,
    the forgiveness of sins,
    the resurrection of the body,
    and the life everlasting. Amen.

## The Lord's Prayer

Our Father, who art in heaven,
    hallowed be thy name;
    thy kingdom come;
    thy will be done on earth as it is in heaven.
    Give us this day our daily bread;
    and forgive us our trespasses
    as we forgive those who trespass against us;
    and lead us not into temptation,
    but deliver us from evil. Amen.

## Hail Mary

Hail Mary, full of grace,
    the Lord is with thee;
    blessed art thou among women,
    and blessed is the fruit of thy womb, Jesus.
    Holy Mary, Mother of God,
    pray for us sinners,
    now and at the hour of our death. Amen.

## Glory Be

Glory be to the Father, and to the Son,
    and to the Holy Spirit,
    as it was in the beginning, is now,
    and ever shall be, world without end. Amen.

Brother **Mickey McGrath** is an Oblate of St. Francis de Sales and an award-winning artist and author. Ever since he can remember he has loved to draw and paint. He thinks that art is a fun and unique way to pray and spread the gospel. His paintings and stories of Jesus, Mary, and the saints have appeared in many books and articles, most notably *Blessed Art Thou*, *At the Name of Jesus*, and *Jesus A to Z*. When he's not painting, Brother Mickey brings the gospel of art to teachers and students of all ages in retreats and presentations throughout the United States.

MARK WINTERBOTTOM

*A note from the artist...*

*Bro. Mickey McGrath*

I am a firm believer in the power of art to help us pray better because art helps our imaginations soar to the heights. Colors and symbols, both traditional and unique, can help us see the presence of God in new ways. So get out your crayons and markers, and draw closer to God!

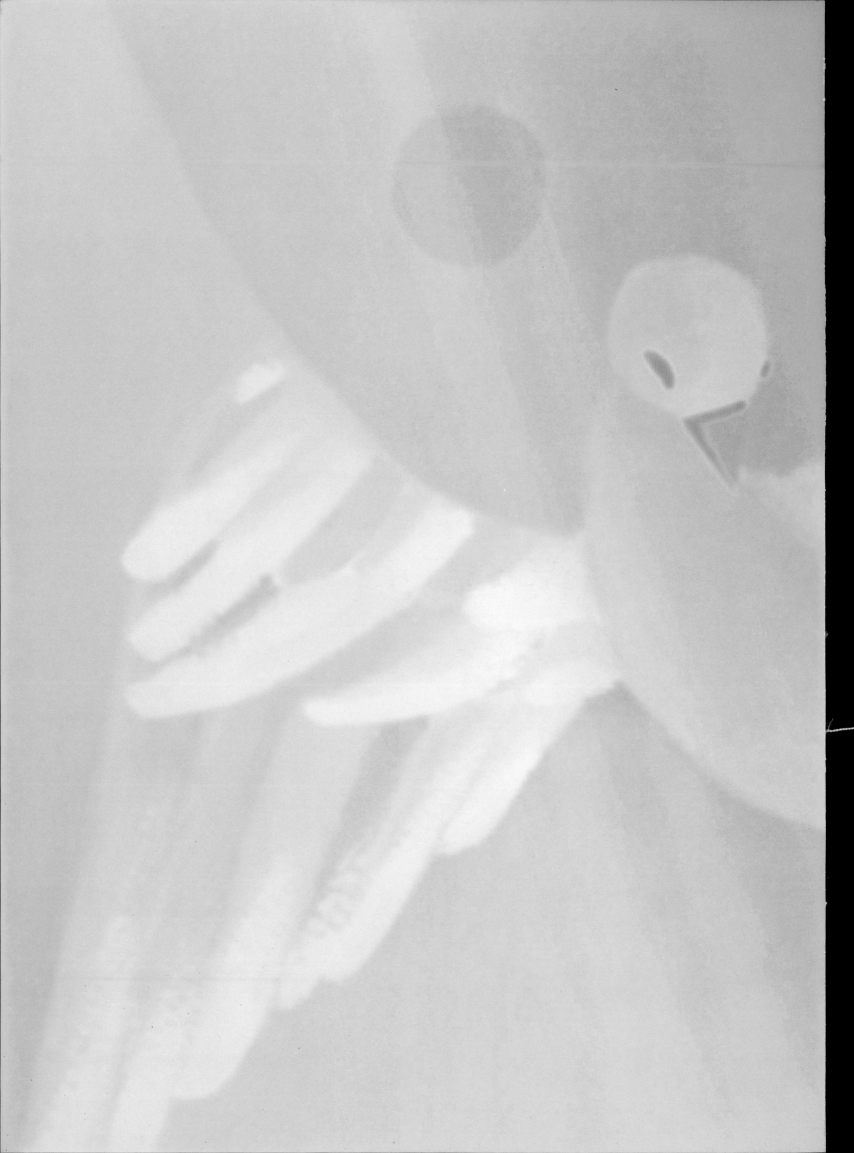